Afterthoughts

Afterthoughts

Kenneth C Calman

Kennedy & Boyd

Kennedy & Boyd
an imprint of
Zeticula Ltd
Unit 13,
196 Rose Street,
Edinburgh,
EH2 4AT,
Scotland

http://www.kennedyandboyd.co.uk
admin@kennedyandboyd.co.uk

First published 2017:
Text Copyright © Kenneth C. Calman 2017
Cover Image: Goatfell mountain on the Island of Arran, taken on
January 2010, from the "Bridge over the River Cloy", the title of
one of the poems © Kenneth C. Calman 2017

ISBN 978-1-84921-170-3

Acknowledgements

It is with pleasure that I acknowledge the support and inspiration for these poems from my family, my friends and my dogs.

A special thanks to Lesley Duncan, Herald (Glasgow) Poetry Editor.

Thanks also to colleagues and friends who have listened or read some of these poems for their very pertinent comments.

Finally, thanks to Professor Tom Gibson, Plastic Surgeon, Past President of the Royal College of Physicians and Surgeons, Glasgow, and poet, for being such a role model to me as a young surgeon.

Contents

Poetry and me

I have always been interested in poetry. The Scottish tradition of children reciting, or singing, at weddings receptions and family events was strong when I was young. My first recorded attempt to write poetry was on a Christmas card I had painted, and addressed to my Aunt Cathie and my Gran. It was subsequently framed in a silver coated cardboard cake plate from which a hole had been cut. It was probably in 1952 when I was ten, and I still have it.

Thereafter the poetry was related to events, such as my 21st birthday invitations and various ones to my girlfriend, subsequently my wife, Ann.

I then used poetry at scientific and medical events, for example "*Ode to the Sebaceous Gland*", was based on my PhD thesis, and delivered at a meeting of the British Dermatological Society.

As a young surgeon I spent a year with Tom Gibson, a very distinguished plastic surgeon and poet, and President of the Royal College of Physicians and Surgeons of Glasgow. A wonderful man whose poem, "*Stratified Squamous Skin*" was the inspiration for my "*Ode to the sebaceous gland*".

Thereafter, I wrote various poems for meetings and events such as "*Ode to Methotrexate*" an anticancer drug, "*From Snoddy to Simon*" on the topic of public health, and others.

It was when we had a dog that things changed, especially with Mungo, a flatcoat retriever and Ailsa, a beagle. Walking through the woods at Durham, where I was based at the time, gave me the opportunity to think, and I always had a note book handy, acting as my Commonplace Book. Subsequently on returning to Glasgow the habit developed further and I became more able to spot a possible poem. These were my "Afterthoughts"

I then prepared for an M.Litt at the University of Glasgow in which I considered the link between Scottish Literature and health and medicine, which was subsequently turned into a book, "*A Doctor's Line*". This made me much more aware of the techniques and power of poetry, by which time I had written around 40 poems, and I thought it might be useful to put them together and to and to build up the collection.

Most of the poems written over the last 15 years have been the result of an observation, and written as an "afterthought" and a reflection on the observation; the inspiration of the event was the source of the poem. Like many poets, I suspect that the poems tell you much about myself, and my own values and feelings. Poems reflect the power of the word and of the story.

They have been about a variety of different issues and I have collected them into groups for convenience. The earliest, presented here, was written in the 1970s and the latest, just a few months before the publication of this volume.

Kenneth C Calman
July 2017.

For Children

Sunshine

The sun is such a nuisance
It lights up all the dust
Its shining ray illuminates
And I really feel I must
Lift on high my duster
Polish some and then
Put the thing away
Until the sun shines again.

2008

The daisy

When the sun is out I feel bold
All my petals I unfold

When the moon is out and it's night
I shut my petals very tight

2013

The robin

The robin is my favourite bird
It follows me around
In amongst the weeds and flowers
As I hoe and till the ground

I love to hear it singing
Its breast so red and soft
We've chatted to one another
Many a time and oft

We're just like old friends
My little pal and me
To have a soul mate is important
Don't you agree?

I need to have a friend
Robin partly fills the bill
Will you be my special friend
Please say that you will?

2013

Sounds of wildlife in Scotland

The coo goes moo
The dove goes coo
Woof goes the dog
Croak-croak goes the frog
The hen goes cluck
And quack goes the duck
But cocks are best for me and you
They loudly cry cock-a-doodle do
The pony went neigh
As she came out to play
The bees go buzz
Making honey for us
You make a wish
When the fish goes swish
Purr goes the cat
As it sits on the mat
The mouse goes squeak
And the seagulls squalk and screech
The wee birds twitter and tweet
Each little one sounds so sweet
Twit twoo goes the owl
Oh dear what a howl
The sheep goes baa
The parrot quacks "ta-ta"
"Thank you folks", and then he'll say
To you and me "Have a nice day"

People

Communication and etiquette

They sat at the table in the pub
Mother, father and two children
The drinks had been served
But they waited for the food

Each had a phone, or a tablet
There was no communication
Not even a nod across the table
No smiles, just eyes on the screens

I wondered what would happen
When the food at last arrived
Would they text to pass the salt?
Or email photos of the food to each other?

Even the youngsters didn't speak
They were engrossed in the machines
And the parents gave no encouragement
To talk and converse, what a pity

Perhaps at home they text
Could I have another slice of toast? or
Can I change the Chanel? or
Put the sound down on your iPad?

Where has etiquette gone?
Not the formal manners of old
But just good manners, like
Talking while breaking bread

Serving hands

Have you ever watched the hands that serve you?
Giving tickets, receipts or change?
Look closely at them next time
There really is a fascinating range.

Some are stubby, rough and flaky
Or red and worn and hard
Others soft and light, sensuous
Some are rather greasy, like lard

Some tremble a little while working
A few have rather a shake
Others show a love of their job
In the movements they make

One who serves me has very delicate hands
They are pale and white and slow
The ticket is laid with precision
He knows exactly where it must go

And then the rings!
And on how many fingers
Nails are varnished or cracked
And this impression lingers

Clutching your bags and purchases
The special offers and the bill
Watch the hands that serve you
Next time you leave the till

And my hands what are they like?
Old, wizened and pale
They once were the hands of a surgeon
Now at that skill, they'd fail

But I can still write a little
And pen a poem, or letter
Not using the knife anymore
Perhaps the word can do better

2014

Magnus Magnusson — A celebration

I lent over and picked the parsley from the terracotta pot
On a glorious June evening on my balcony
I ground it, chewed it, tasted it on its own; free from fish,
    soup and stew
Its green leaves full of vitality

Earlier we had celebrated the life of Magnus
In an intoxicating and emotional mixture of words and music
He too was fresh, green and full of vitality. Glorious on his own,
Yet adding flavour and zest to all whom he touched

I keep my copy of Culpepper's Herbal at my bedside
My "Chambers" is not under my bed as Magnus professed
My random picking of parsley was prescient and propitious,
Under the dominion of Mercury; the winged messenger,
    the bringer of stories

As the Great Hero, Beowolf, once unlocked his word-hoard
So Magnus unlocked his in a multitude of ways
To enlighten us all with news, histories and sagas
A master mind with a master's command of words

The green shreds of parsley clung to my teeth
And stayed with me all evening as I read on my balcony.
The sun set on the day as I looked south and west
Leaving me with my dreams and remembrances.

The Leaving

The words and Accent were foreign to me
But the body language and signs were not
As she waved goodbye to her little boy
Her husband standing by him
As she ascended the elevator
She gave waves and kisses in abundance
A tear in her eye revealed her emotion
And was reflected in her sparkling earrings
But still she kept waving until out of sight
And into the security hall
A small episode in a large terminal
Flying away from a loved one
And I was flying home.
Ten years ago he would have left her and the boy.
How things have changed.

26 March 2011

Thanks to Bill

The year was noughty-five I'm sure
When Bill Bryson did arrive
His reputation gone before him,
"Take my car", he said "and drive"!

So he came to Durham
And was escorted through the town
As the students met his train
To a Varsity of renown

His humour, his humanity
Shone through his Chancellor's remit
As he spoke in the Cathedral
Full of commonsense and wit

He likes to keep the city
Looking clean and neat
No rubbish on the pavement
No rubbish on the street

We support his endeavour
And did our best, after a fashion
It is his lasting legacy
As is his erudition and compassion

He really suited that red gown
And his white and silky jabot
He represented us with dignity
He's a man you'd want to know

Thank you Bill for being
A Chancellor so fine
And for giving us your wisdom
Your energy and time

We will miss you greatly
And I personally regret
Your leaving of Durham
You're a man we won't forget

We wish you all the best
For us you've done so much
Good health, success and happiness
I hope we keep in touch

2012

Well-dressed on holiday

There's a place I go on holiday
It's rather nice you see
'Cause even on the beach
Well dressed you have to be

Dunlop shorts, Adidas shoes
A special kind of sweat shirt
Casual shirts, with real pockets
And never a trace of dirt

Imagine the scene when into the town
Came a man to stay at his grannies
He was wearing a Buck's Fizz tea shirt
And was sporting black socks and sannies.

2012

The airport

I'm sitting alone at the airport, my flight is late again
Inside the airport is bustling, outside it looks like rain

I feel tense, anxious, excited, it's not flying that
     engenders the fear
It the fact that an aeroplane's sitting out there
     and home seems ever so near

Children are crying, trolleys trundle by
And all I want to do is get up there and fly

Once more I see the shops, buy more than I should
Another cup of coffee, another bite of food

The tannoy booms out loudly, another hour to wait
What will happen in another hour? what will be my fate?

Some think that travel's glamorous full of kicks
     and thrills
I'd rather be at home or walking on the hills

The sun peeps through, is it a sign? I put away my pen
Soon I'll be home with the family, until the travel
     starts again

2012

A short back and sides

I've had lots of fun in my life
And lots more besides
But none are quite as restful
As a short back and sides

For 10 minutes or so I do nothing
No telephones and no chides
I sit and relax and enjoy
While he starts my short back and sides

Mike, my Barber, talks to me
Indeed he quite often confides
He tells me lots of gossip
While I have a short back and sides

He covers local politics
As around my chair he glides
I listen, but don't interrupt
As I get my short back and sides

And then we get to football
And I mustn't take sides
When he gives me his position
As he continues my short back and sides

Because of my advancing years
Just like my free bus rides
My payment is reduced a bit
To complete my short back and sides

The others who sit there waiting
Contribute their thoughts and asides
And raise a laugh or cry
While I get my short back and sides

The process carries on apace
Ye can't stop time or tides
It has to finish sometime
My short back and sides

We shake hands on parting
The Karma we share coincides
And I say I will come again soon
For another short back and sides

My barber is my hero
As is the craft in which he bides
He gives more than just a haircut
And a short back and sides.

Worshipful Company of Barbers
25 January 2016

Dog walkers

They are a breed part, the walkers that is
They meet in parks, the seaside, on hills
Their dress sense determined by weather
And not by fashion or frills

The talk when they meet is about dogs
Whose names are generally weel kent
But not the names of the walkers
Whose time is rather better spent

There is no class with dog walkers
All on a level, no discussion of jobs whatsoever
Or politics or news, but rather
The foxes, the deer, and the weather

The dogs run in packs after balls and sticks
And while the owners discuss the importance of vets
The dogs sniff the grass, and roll in mud
And the walkers converse about pets

Some of the dogs are expensive of course
Others mutts, with no pedigree
Some are from charities or homes
All loved to the same degree

Which takes us to the dress sense again
It should be resilient, dark, easily washed
Boots, wellies or heavy shoes
Funny waterproof hats that look rather squashed

Poo bags in every pocket
At least one in every suit
Embarrassing when trying to get a hanky out
At a dinner party or meeting, what a hoot!

The camaraderie is palpable
Greetings are exchanged, good wishes sent
Always asking for the dog and any stories
New diets to try, time well spent

They meet at all times of the day
Morning, noon and night
Though the dress sense rarely changes
They still look a terrible sight

There are times I like to be alone
Just Ailsa, my wee beagle, and me
My note book and pen and my thoughts
To walk, and compose, and be free

I'm glad that I'm a dog walker
I like to go out and meet others
It takes me away from mundane skills
To celebrate my dogs with other dog lovers

January 2014

Breakfast

A young couple having breakfast together
Not unusual you might think
But they were outside, and it was cold
Snow was in the air and they looked vulnerable
The breakfast was hearty enough
High fibre, fresh fruit
But it still looked cold
They were busy eating away
When the dog disturbed them
And the two blackbirds flew away
And returned to the fallen apples later
To finish the meal

2008

Listening and learning

Speaking up

The meeting dragged on endlessly, key issues
    not addressed
Speakers pontificated, their neighbours not impressed
Boredom settled in, eyelids shutting fast
Should I speak up now, or should my silence last?
Do it now!

I jotted down responses, scribbled little notes
Clarified my thinking, thought of suitable quotes
I took every opportunity to make my opinions known
I was clearly with the minority, out there on my own
Can I do it now?

Courage, brother do not stumble, rattled through my head
Perhaps I should not speak now, have a coffee instead
I was sweating just a little, pulse rate elevated
I collected my scraps of paper, finally elated
And I spoke

Surprisingly my faltering words, found some sympathy
Members nodded knowingly, evidence of empathy
My confidence grew, and I spoke with feeling
I spoke with passion and to emotions appealing
And I'm glad I spoke

The moral of this story is always speak your mind
It might just surprise you how much resonance you'll find

2008

The heron

I watched the heron from through the trees
It stood still silent, head erect
A sophisticated bird, who, every now and then
    straightened its tie
Checked its fly, smoothed its shirt, and breathed deeply
Such wonderful deportment.
Ardea cinerea, the grey heron.
I christened him Augustus.
In flight its chest puffed out
Like a guardsman on parade.
Sometimes on the bank, sometimes on the rock
Sometimes in the water, its feet must be freezing
While the noise in Glasgow surrounded the pond
Lorries, machines and my dog barking
Didn't disturb its concentration
I watched and wondered if I could do the same
Be still, reflective, fishing
And watch the world rather than the e-mails
The dog called me to attention
And I left the heron, still silent, and still
Two hours later I returned
To find the heron still there, unmoved by the
    sounds of the city
It had remained there, beautiful, erect,
Thinking, and watching, and fishing
As if to strengthen this train of thought.
A few days later I visited the Burrell Collection
And in that bright and airy courtyard with the Warwick Vase
Was Rodin's "The Thinker". Could I do it?

Could I just sit and think, and "fish in my mind".
Be reflective and both inward and outward looking
And consider where I had got to, and where I would go?
So I did it. I really did it.
Now presumably the heron has a plan, to scan the pond
And looks for sounds and sight in the black water
I too would need a plan to help me fish in my mind
I couldn't sit for 2 hours staring at the ceiling
The heron's meditation had a purpose
So what was mine, did I really have one?
The catechism came back to me
Man's chief end is to glorify God.
Should I rehearse my career so far?
Think of my relationships with family friends and
        colleagues?
Consider my philosophy of life and living?
This life, up until now, had been simple;
Enjoy the little things in life
Making every day count
Adjust expectations up and down.
That was done, something else was needed, but what?
Decisions, decisions, decisions.
Later, perhaps three weeks later,
I saw another heron fly slowly and majestically
Across Brodick bay, his island cousin
Could I think better on Arran?
Let it all hang out. I had a vision of my cerebrum drooping
And a hippocampus hanging
As I watched Goatfell from my room.

2008

27

Meetings

When people ask me what I do
I say I attend committees
There is some surprise at this response
As well as sighs and pities

What does that mean, they say?
What do you do in committees?
Well, I travel all around the world
Meeting in different cities

Meetings are good, they pass the time
I take notes in my diary and jotter
I sometimes use my iPad
But I know I shouldn't oughter

One thing I try, not to do
And I know I am not alone
Is to check at regular intervals
My texts and emails by phone

I try not to respond, but it's hard
I hold the phone just under the table
I try to reply unobtrusively
But sometimes I'm just not able

I talk and I listen, read lots of paper
Eat biscuits, drink coffee and tea
I always fill in my expenses form
Meetings are costly, you see

It's different of course if the meeting you chair
You must be alert and awake
You must let everyone speak, not too long
And sides you should not take

You must sum the points for action
The time line and costs agreed
The minutes and the final report written up
To be implemented with all speed

Some reports are indeed taken forward
They seem to strike a chord
Others just languish on a shelf
Sunk without even a word

But....
Meetings, meetings, I love them
Better than squash or a jog
But perhaps not as good as reading a book
Or going a walk with the dog.

21 August 2012

Missed connections

Two days of missed connections made me think.
Planes and trains late, Late for meetings and late home.
Did it matter? Not in the great scheme of things
The delay and lost opportunities
But tiring and annoying.

Made me think of other missed connections.
People not connected with, books not read,
Knowledge unaware of, places not seen.
Could they have been avoided?
And did they matter?

Impossible to say at this distance,
Not like the immediate problem of transport.
Maybe they would have changed my life.
Could I have avoided the missed connections?
Let me think

Could I have turned up earlier
Or packed more into each day?
Should I have e-mailed more?
Or used the Internet more effectively?
To ensure connections.

If I had tried harder, worked longer
Would it have made a difference?
Then I remembered that Old Scots saying
"Whit's fur Ye will no go by Ye"
And I relaxed.

I was not meant to meet these other people
To make connections unknown
I did not need to work as hard
I should just have enjoyed myself.
Or should I? Perhaps I did.

When the work week starts

The weather man said, "when the work week starts"
And I was amazed and perplexed. A week in parts?
The concept of work having a beginning and an end
Seemed strange, not quite right, did he wish to offend?
From Monday to Friday, would it work for you?
What to do at weekends? With no work to do?
Who would answer the phone? Check each email and text?
Get the writing completed. What will they think of next?
They will soon be saying work goes from 9.00 to 5.00
On weekdays, with the evenings, free to skive
What a world to live in, a world work free
He should wake up in the real world, then he would see!

2013

Personal

A suburban garden

Myosotis, did you notice, is a rather delicate blue
Convallaria majalis, white bells perfume the dew
Sorbus aucuparia, berries whisper in the wind, upright
Erica carnea or *vulgaris*, purple hills and lucky white

Your dark brown eyes I will not forget
Nor your quiet murmurings and your support
Nor your fragrance as I walk beside you
My home with you and my good fortune

2010

The moon and us

I winked at the moon, and the moon winked back
And I thought of your freshness and promise
I smiled at the full moon, mellow and bright
I recalled your laughter and warmness

I talked to the moon, sharp through the frost
I remembered your knowledge and wit
I sighed at the misty moon, close and mysterious
And enjoyed your softness and spirit

It may seem strange to talk of winking and laughing
I know I don't do it alone
I know that you also look at the moon
It's become our celestial phone.

2008

How did I get here?

The fourth of July, an auspicious date
Damp and humid, as I stand on the red carpet
It is Glasgow, George Square, and the year 2012
The diamond Jubilee of the Queen.
Here I was waiting to greet her Majesty and the Duke
As Deputy Lieutenant, standing with the Lord Provost
On their visit to my home City.
As the crowds watched me, and waved
Anticipating the cavalcade of cars sweeping in
It occurred to me to ask, how did I get here?
It was a special moment for me and I almost cried.
My life began 70 years ago, in a council house
My old school a few hundred yards away,
And yet here I was greeting the Queen!
What was the path, the journey, which lead to this task?
The story is a very personal one, filled with lots of
        small stories
And against a backdrop of huge changes in the world.
But it is one that might benefit from telling....some day

Blindness restored

The demise of the telephone box

In the beginning red boxes were my life line
  With their neat windows to the street and sky
  And telephone wires to you

And it came to pass, from pub nooks
  Tube station niches, hotel desks
  I used them all to call you

Next, the revelation, a liberating mobile phone
  Free to call you anytime, any where
  Imprint your voice on my own electronic circuits

Finally, the apocalypse, blind spots between buildings
  Tedious tunnels, a failed call, contact cut
  Senseless satellite, losing you, missing you

A revival please, bring back my red rock
  And with it your soft voice
  I need you both too much

2008

Do I seem old?

It's happened twice now.
Once on a bus and once on the tube.
I have been asked if I needed a seat.
I declined both, with grace
Then I wondered
Do I seem old?

I have no stick
I walked on without stumbling
I had a heavy bag, but managed
So what was it that I showed?
My wrinkled Face? My anxious looks?
Did they make me look old?

Both my questioners
Were being kind and thoughtful
They were willing to give up their seat
To help me. I was grateful
But it made me wonder
If I did really look old.

20 May 2014

A perfect evening on Skye

We arrived on the ferry from Mallaig
Having visited Glencoe and Glenfinnan
The hotel was at a sea loch
And the weather perfect, but cold
As we strolled around we realised
That there was no phone reception
No telephone, just perfect

After supper in the bar another stroll
Checked at the hotel reception, no wifi
Then to our room up creaking stairs
And we then discovered, no television
No telephone, no television, just perfect
We read, books, newspapers in peace
No telephone, no television, just books, just perfect

As the night darkened, lights out at 10.15
We slept and snuggled in together
And realised that no dog kept us apart
Ailsa was missing and we were alone together
Just as it had been over 40 years ago
On the same island, Skye, on our honeymoon
With no telephone, no television, no beagle, bed early
Just books, and a wee cuddle. Just perfect

But I miss them all, but for one evening,
Just perfect

2012

Is that it?

A happy upbringing
Though lost my father early
Lovely wife and family
And now a grandfather
Lots of friends and great colleagues
A glittering academic career
Chairman of organisations
Committees and commissions
At home and abroad
A knighthood and honours
And now at seventy,
Is that it?

What's left for me
Or am I now finished
Nothing ahead of me
But pottering in the garden,
Reading my books
And visiting the family?
Nothing else to go for?
What will be my next adventure?
Would my autobiography do?
What about my poetry?
I could still remain the teacher, a leader
The future of Scotland still excites me
It is still my country

And then the chest pain came and the priorities changed

Health and Medicine

Address to medical students

There will come a time when it will be up to you.
In front of you sits a person
Who seeks your help, your care, your compassion.
You will draw on all your experiences
Of teachers, books, resources, past patients
To answer, assist, help this individual
All the anatomy, physiology, pathology, therapeutics you know
Is focussed on the problem; but remember
This is a person, with feelings, emotions, anxieties
Waiting to be listened to and be understood.
More than a collection of bones, muscles, cells
An individual, a whole person, a human being with a soul
With a family, friends, a home, a job, or not
The social context of the illness needs similar concern
That's where you matter. Making all this come together
The synthesis, the diagnosis, not in any limited
            biomedical sense
But as a process of integrating all those factors which
            matter to them
With one purpose in mind, and with your professionalism,
To care for the person in front of you
To help them on their journey to restoration of health
Or to be with them on a different road to comfort and care
And share the pain
That's what all this learning is for,
And that time is now.

2004

I'm feeling peely wally

I'm just a wee bit wabbit
Not enough to make me crabbitt
But I feel I need a sleep

I waken early in the morning
Before the day is dawning
And I can't get back to sleep

I've tried lots of pills and potions
And aromatic lotions
But still I canny sleep

I've tried the demon drink
And it hardly makes me blink
I really canny sleep

Problems run around my brain
My neurons seem to take the strain
I wish I just could sleep

Counting sheep's a waste of time
I always get them all in line
And yet I canny sleep

The snoring is a problem though
It's the dog, not the wife, you know
It doesn't help me sleep

I've tried the windae open, shut
Two pillows and no duvet, but
Still I canny sleep

I've tried it hot, I've tried it cold
Believe you me, if truth be told
Nothing helps me sleep

So what's the answer to my deprivation
Can I find a cure, a resolution.
What really will help me sleep?

And then I go to Arran and everything comes right
A walk on the beach, some golf. and see the stars at night
Then at last I sleep.

Counting as the weeks go by.

It's usually on a Sunday night that the counting
      commences
How this week has passed brings me to my senses
Neatly, into the special box, I drop each potent pill
I reflect upon the week gone by and how each day I fill
First, I'm still alive, so the pills must work for me
I hope they keep on functioning, I've lots still to do
      and see
Last week was very busy, each day I seemed to fill
Solving little problems, no time to just be still
Took the dog for walks, checked each and every email
Went to lots of meetings and listened without fail
I had lunches and dinners, far too much I'm sure
Need to cut back soon, and help the pills effect their cure
Now the pills are counted, checked, I could almost sing
Another week gone by; what will the next one bring?

2013

48

My first time

A discovery of a short typed operation note
On yellow paper reminded me
And took me back to my first time
It began with a brief recognition under bright lights
Our hands touched gently, and I could feel her relaxing
Too early in the day for this intimacy
The ritual cleansing for both of us began
She was now completely relaxed
I was tense, for my first time
I was delicate at first, then, as my confidence grew
I became more forceful
The whole thing did not last more than 30 minutes
When she woke she had some stabbing pain
But was pleased it had happened.
Later, at night, we sat and held hands, and talked
I saw her three weeks later, her mastectomy stitches
            removed
She looked great, and wanted to talk about the future.
The bond between surgeon and patient, secured

27 April 2010

Patient-centred care

The topic for the symposium was given to me
I did not choose it and I wasn't sure, you see.
And what would I say?
What does it mean anyway?
And from where would I get my inspiration
Other than from the patients I have cared for
Over the years?

I went first to my medical cartoon collection
And there I saw on my recollection
Insensitive interviews, clumsy communication
Dominant doctors, poor use of words
And inappropriate body language
All amusing in their own way, but very serious
And what painful lessons

And then to my next love, my literature notes,
And the views of writers and poets. And their quotes
Some poems exalt the doctor who is wonderful
And does everything right, loved by patients.
Others demonstrate their weaknesses and follies.
For myself as doctor with a special interest in cancer
Some poems and readings are especially powerful

How should we tell the truth?
Listen to Dumbledore, he's not aloof
As he addresses Harry Potter.
"The truth" Dumbledore sighed,
"it is a beautiful and a terrible thing,
And should be treated with great caution.
However ....I shall not of course lie"

So how can patient-centred care be ratified?
With a process, which leaves the patient and family satisfied,
Happy with their care and decisions taken
Centred on the person who matters most
Involving patients in the decisions
Listening to their concerns, exploring the options
Deciding together.

So how do I learn to care in this way?
First, from patients, we heed what they say
Who have given me so much to learn.
Their experiences and their wish to help others
Including the doctor
Then from personal experiences over the years in practice,
In surgery, oncology and public health

We don't always get it right, but we can learn.
And their respect we need to earn
In medicine, nursing and the other health professions.
These have been especially powerful for me,
Both good and bad.
Textbooks and journal articles can help
But practical experience and testing the theory, is crucial

But what if the decision doesn't seem right?
How is that to be taken forward? Is it worth a fight?
Whose opinion matters most?
An ethical dilemma is presented
A difficult clinical situation with no easy solutions
More discussion, more debate, another clinical opinion
May help, but at the end of the day it is the patient who
matters.

Finally, can all this experience be refined
And brought together in a few succinct lines?
Probably not, but let's try.
First, a passion for people and to do the best for them
Motivated by love
Second, to see patient-centred care as a value,
And part of my professional duty and responsibilities

The values of the Hippocratic Oath, founded
To treat all equally, do no harm, on which they are grounded.
To listen to patients and learn from them
To welcome them to the surgery or clinic
And with care and compassion, skills and experience
Create an ambience, with attention to detail.

As Kahil Gibran says, and see how the quotation rings,
"For it is in the dew of little things
That the heart finds its morning and is refreshed"
To improve satisfaction, happiness,
Well-being and quality of life
And to practice from the heart,
As well as the head.

This does not mean that cure can be achieved
Or that symptoms and signs will always be relieved
They may not
But that all avenues have been explored
The patient in control of the process, right at the centre.
This includes a wide range of therapies
With an emphasis on emotional and practical care

Burns was right in the Epistle to Davie
"If happiness hae not her seat, An centre in the breast
We may be wise, or rich, or great, But never can be blest!
Nae treasures or pleasures
Could make us happy lang
The heart aye's the part aye
That makes us right or wrang".

Let us see happiness, quality of life and well-being
As goals in medicine, far seeing
Given freely by a wide range of staff
Volunteers, helpers, therapists of all sorts
It is our responsibility to "tak tent", to take care
Of those who entrust themselves to us.
That is our responsibility

5 October 2014

Akrasia

"Always use the handrail and take care on the stairs"
The voice boomed and the notices shouted.
I sometimes do, but not always.
As you get older such things matter
Indeed, I could have written it myself
As could my wife for me.
I should slow down, take more care
And look after myself

Why don't we? Why can we not do it?
The old word for it is Akrasia —
Knowing what's wrong, but still doing it.
And it's not just about handrails or stairs,
It's food, exercise, the drink and smoking
To name but a few. As Burns said
"The moving why we do it",
And yet we regret it.

Is it stress which makes us do it?
Too much on our minds to think of such things?
Other decisions too important?
And divert our actions away from our health?
Do I have the wrong priorities?
Or do too many other things get in the way?
Short term satisfaction and forget
The long term problems and priorities?

We want to live better and feel better
Enjoy life more, be happier

And we can. We can use the handrails
And take care on the stairs,
We can live better, and I should slow down,
Take things easy, But I have so much to do
And the handrail is cold
And the stairs are still easy to climb

Envy

He stood beside me
Tall slim and muscular
He had hair, lots of it
I was small, stooping
And a little overweight
And I was bald

His skin was smooth
Clear and shiny
Mine was dry and flaky
With lots of blotches
His hands firm
Mine thin and shaky

But the real difference
Was in the noise
As the liquid stream
Hit the white basin
And the length of time
The stream lasted

Mine took time to start
It was weak and I dribbled
He was able to stop.
My stream was hesitant
And I stood almost in silence
Trying hard

How I envied him!

And the boy on the other side
Reminded me
Of school days
And how far up the wall
My stream would go.
What I used to be
Now a shadow

My envy deepened!

And all because of a tiny gland
This, I hope you will understand
The prostate grows when you grow old
Hence the story I've just told

Of envy

The lost quadrant

New Year's day. The afternoon is frosty, bright
The car is full, five adults, tight
The sun is low and the visor down
Along the expressway east into town

Suddenly, no warning given, a shadow in my right eye
The upper quadrant, like the slice of a pie
I keep on driving with a patch of fuzzy grey
Couldn't tell anyone, what would I say?

Parked the car, let every one go inside
Stayed behind and wished I could confide
Then suddenly it vanished, my sight was clear
Was it an embolus, vascular spasm, did I need to fear?

Was it the start of a degenerative process?
Blood vessels thickening, or early thrombosis?
The start of the year had begun rather badly
I mused as I drove home, slowly and sadly

I'd played party games, eaten my fill
But, without pleasure and against my will
What did it mean, was it a portent?
That life might change, certainly important

Was it a signal, was it an inkling?
A temporary illusion, to shape my thinking?
The year ahead will reveal, might tell
    And I thought of you

2008

I felt old today

I really felt old today, inside and out
My bones and joints were creaking
And my skin was wrinkled,
My fingers stiff and
I was tired and listless
And walking seemed difficult
My legs were like lead, I picked at my food
Yesterday was different. I rushed around,
Too much to do
Writing and phoning, and on the laptop.
What changed? Was it something inside?
Will it last, or was this a premonition of how it will be?

Architecture and healing

Many years ago when I was at school, I wanted to be an architect. Mainly, I suppose, because Charles Rennie MacIntosh had been a pupil there. But I changed and became interested in the architecture of the body. However, I have always maintained an interest, and, in particular, in the relevance of architecture to healing, in clinical settings. This wee poem sets out some of my thoughts.

The practice of Architecture is real
With buildings you can touch and feel
These bring to us form and space
And to all of us a sense of place
      Architecture matters to all our lives

Architecture can influence healing
To body, mind and soul appealing
Those hospitals, surgeries, clinics which arise
Need careful planning and be pleasant to the eyes
      Architecture can help us all

The evidence suggests that Healing is best,
In buildings which are designed as places of rest
Peace to think and reflect, in times of strife
And to meditate on well-being and quality of life
      We can all feel better

Not crowded clinics, with no privacy about
And no confidentiality as names are read out
How space is used, the role of the arts
A place of tranquillity and of mending hearts
      Dignity is essential

These "Castles of Healing", no matter where
Are vital to us all, to assist in patient care
They are so important to staff who work with passion
To improve the outcome with care and compassion
A special thanks to our architects.

Gaudeamus igitur

Gaudeamus Igitur, seniores dum sumus
We looked back across the square to the castle
Heidelberg's great ornament, and the guide said
Remember the Student Prince and hear the students,
Carousing and Singing *Gaudeamus Igitur*

It took me back in nostalgia to my student days
            in Glasgow
A university 70 years younger than Heidelberg
Where I first learned the words and the music
And they flooded back again, with the memories

And more recent ones too, at graduations
Where the words are sung by the students
As the academic procession comes into the great hall,
Relatives and friends listening and joining in

Gaudeamus Igitur — therefore let us rejoice
While we are still young, with energy and ideals
And as we get older the troubles of age appear
We know that soon we will return to the earth

Here, as I stood in the square, I wondered
About these words and their meaning
Is it really true that age brings troubles?
I beg to disagree! Is it not also a time for hope and joy?

Age brings its own rewards and happiness
It generates its own ideas and thoughts
You can still have energy and excitement
And all life's lessons learned can help

Gaudeamus igitur, seniores dum sumus
Gaudeamus igitur, vivamus floreamus
Let us therefore rejoice, we have reached old age
Therefore, let us rejoice and enjoy it!

Another verse praises academia
And that they should live long and flourish
Now that I agree with and support!
But the heart remains, *Gaudeamus Igitur*

Whether we are young or old
Life is to be enjoyed to the full
Student or professor, ideals matter
Gaudemaus igitur, vivamus floreamus

Successors to Snoddy and Simon

Dr Snoddy was a fictional character in A.J.Cronin's novels, short
stories, and TV and radio adaptations, such as *Dr. Findlay's Casebook*.
Dr. John Simon (1816-1904) was the first Chief Medical Officer of
England (1855-1876).

Public health is good fun, it deals with populations,
Prevention, and screening and public expectations.
History is rich in people to keep an eye on
And tonight we represent the successors to Snoddy
    and Simon.

It's interesting to reflect on past achievements
    and traditions
But it's no good just reflecting, we need to have ambitions
'Cause the population out there needs someone to rely on –
That's us, you know, the Successors to Snoddy and Simon.

Perhaps the first great pioneer was Thomas Sydenham
His clinical studies were where it all began,
And maybe there's a lesson, I'll identify it if I may —
We need to get close to where the people are today.

This emphasises links with colleagues clinical
In general practice or in the hospital.
Academic public health must also integrate
The benefits enormous, the consequences great.

Jenner's work on cowpox, Blossom's name will live,
Illustrates another point - I hope you will forgive
If I quote the words of Hunter in a letter Ed received,
He said "Try, don't think", let us see what you've achieved

There followed some distinguished sanitary men —
Duncan, Simon, Littlejohn, all are in our ken.
Remember the High Street, Edinburgh — a tenement
    crumbles,
"I'm no' deid yet", the little boy mumbles.

And we're no deid yet either, we have lots of work to do.
The Network is a start, for me and I hope for you.
Intelligence for health, and the search for clues,
Takes us back to Medical Police, not the first name
    I would choose.

Intelligence means action, and we must have a solution
For communicable disease and environmental pollution.
It means good communication, perhaps by Epinet,
By fax or phone our needs will thus be met.

The early pioneers were scientists through and through,
We should not hesitate to join them and be scientists too.
Without the knowledge base, progress will be slow.
Action is determined by what we really know.

We need to get the data to show what really matters,
Otherwise our policies will be left in tatters.
It's not just epidemiology, or even sociology,
But genetics, pathology and molecular biology.

Snoddy is a caricature, an administrator to the core.
We needn't look too far back to see what was in store
If we hadn't changed and seen the sanitary light
We would have been left behind - not a pretty sight.

We really do need action, not further bits of paper,
Thus bureaucratic quagmire may seem like just a caper.
We have serious work to do, we've targets to attain,
We know where we are going, the objective – Health Gain.

Effectiveness and outcomes, we go on lots of courses
To help us best to maximise our finite resources.
Audit is one way to be self-critical,
With peer review besides, it's not just theoretical.

Comparative results, league tables by the score,
Standards and guidelines, good practice galore;
The cornerstone is quality, that's how it all began
To continually improve, and do the best we can.

We have a specialty that's open to public participation —
Essential if we are to improve the Health of the Nation.
We need the public voice, it's their health after all,
We'll strengthen our position if we on them call.

They're on our side, remember, the public health
          comes first,
They're part of the system, for better or for worse.
They're our natural allies, we should try to bring them in.
If we do that, I'm sure that improvement will begin.

The early pioneers began a very fine tradition,
Annually they produced a work of erudition —
The Annual Report — even more important now,
Detailing health needs — the what, and the how.

Reports themselves are not enough, they need an action base
To keep up the momentum with energy and pace.
Reports provide the opportunity to promote the
        primacy of health
And relate to the social system and the generation of wealth.

Simon and Duncan were in there at the start,
They recognised that health care was only just a part
Of improving health; other things were needed —
Housing, environment — and in some they succeeded

We must do likewise, the problems are the same,
But with energy and enthusiasm we can play the game.
We must take up the challenge and clarify the vision,
And we must achieve it; that must be our mission.

We need to set the vision, we need to look ahead,
Not just at the organisation or even how it's led,
But at values, principles and purpose; we must not
        be myopic.
Therefore I present to you my thoughts upon this topic.

Public health is about improving the common weal,
Health, quality of life and how people really feel
About themselves and their communities, in a safe
        environment
With justice and equity and measure of content.

Health of the Nation targets show us where to aim,
Some are easy, some are hard, not all are the same.
Take smoking cigarettes - there's no use in us disguising
That things would be much easier if we stopped all
advertising.

Accidents, mental health and sexually transmitted
    diseases —
They're much more important than simple coughs and
    sneezes.
They're difficult to tackle, whether you're a woman or
    a man,
And remember — use a sunscreen, if you want a tan.

Teenage pregnancies and suicides are a sign of some
    concern.
Is there something missing, something we should learn?
Society has responsibility to assist those most in need,
To nurture and empower and help them to succeed

Health promotion can be difficult, behaviour's not easy
    to change,
We need more effective measures, we need to expand
    the range.
Perception of health is crucial, as Kant said from afar,
"We see things not as they are, but as we are".

Black and ethnic minorities are a very special case,
They have specific problems which we must really face.
They need to be dealt with sensitively, for him as well as her,
Involvement is essential for improvements to occur.

For me the key to change is professional education,
And if I concentrate on doctors, please forgive my
    peroration.
Medical education is a continuum, from student to CME,
Education is a life-long process, for you folks and for me.

The curriculum may need to change, health to emphasise,
And public health, ethics, values and how to organise
And manage health and systems of health care
And communicate and listen to let people know
     we're there

We need continually our skills to develop and to hone
And audit our performance, based on outcomes that
     we own.
Quality is paramount, we need to be the best,
The public is expecting it, that will be the test.

So Health for All's not a slogan, it's a concept and a goal,
It envisages health for everyone, for the population as
     a whole.
Emotive words like equity, social class and deprivation
Are what needs to be tackled to achieve Health of
     the Nation.

The time for dreaming, introspection, navel gazing
     now has gone.
Public health looks forward to a new and sparkling dawn.
So as you sit there relaxing with a therapeutic toddy,
Remember you're the successor to Simon and Snoddy.

1998. Written on the eve of my retiral as CMO England.

Scotland and the wider world

When the battle's o'er.... it's Scotland that matters

Come September 2014......
When the votes have been cast,
Counted, and the result announced
One side will have won and the other lost
And the Nation divided.
But Scotland's future is more important
Than personal pride and ambition
Scotland needs all of us
To be a full and effective force
We all must be included
         And pull together for Scotland's sake

Those who backed independence
Should welcome talent from a' the airts
Those who supported the Union
Must also bring in all the expertise
Without this, the Nation will be split in two
And Healing will be needed.
Some means must be found
To re-establish our country
With the ambition to become one again
And all work for Scotland
         Because it's Scotland that matters most

Who wins and who loses
Will determine the future
For the winner, the road is clear; either
The move to negotiations for independence,
Or the challenge of more devolution or federalism

But what if your cause is lost?
Where will your responsibilities lie?
The Edinburgh agreement made it clear
The winner will be respected.
And all agreed to support the will of the people
Because Scotland comes first

Our leaders need to commit
To use all the talents in our Nation.
And the obverse is true
Those whose dreams have been shattered
Should not sulk for too long
They must want to contribute
And move towards reconciliation
And look ahead to expand
Our place in the world
And achieve a better Scotland
And brithers be for a' that

At Bannockburn's Rotunda, Kathleen Jamie writes
"Come all ye" the Country says,
"You win me, who take me most to heart."
This is our country. It belongs to all of us
And all our hearts need to be thirled to its future.
And I have the "audacity to hope",
To use the words I heard recently,
That the differences between us will be put aside
And Scotland will rise, whoever wins,
And be a united Nation again
And now the battle's o'er...it's Scotland that really
matters

2013. Written before the Referendum on Scottish Independence,
18th September 2014

My Scotland

If I had to begin my story somewhere
It would here on Arran.
I stand on Brodick Bay looking east
With Mungo swimming like a seal
The soft sand beneath my feet
Close to where Bruce sailed for Turnberry
And then on to Bannockburn,
I see Ayrshire and the ferry
Through the afternoon haze.
In my mind's eye I travel to the east
St Andrews, Arbroath, Aberdeen.
Edinburgh sits there in its splendour
Home of Parliament, seat of Government
And a Nation in evolution
Debating and confronting devolution
And from the west, and from the hills
I can see the Paps of Jura, the Antrim Coast
And the setting sun
Onwards up the Great Glen to Inverness
And to the Isles where the language of Eden is spoken
Tir nan Og
The stones of Machrie Moor linking to
The great stones of Callanish on Lewis
From the north I can see Ben Lomond
And the Firth of Clyde, whose river
Has been the birthplace of the world's ships
And on to Stirling and Perth
To the mountains of the north, and the glory
Of the northern Viking isles
From Goatfell I can be seen from Glasgow
On the shore at Lochranza I can gaze

At Hutton's unconformity
And the birth of geology
MacDiarmid's words haunt me.
"What happens to us is irrelevant to the world's geology
What happens to the world's geology
Is not irrelevant to us"
I watch the climate change
And our environment morphing
MacDiarmid again:
"Earth thou bonny brookit bairn"
South I look to the borders
The Solway and the tweed
And Hadrian's wall; the great divide.

I have covered the place
And skimmed its history
But does my story stop here?
Is Scotland just a place on the map?
A small but beautiful country
Rough, gentle, barren, fertile, green, brown, blue
Worth visiting to taste the whisky, adore the bagpipes
And to take photos of men in kilts
Is that it? Is this my Scotland?

Of course not!
For me it begins with the people of Scotland
And how they live their lives.
My quality of life links to books, work,
The first tee at Brodick, papermaking,
Walking with Mungo,
And the people I love.
I have been lucky; education liberated me

As it has countless others.
My forebears toiled in the fields,
In Perthshire, Fife and Angus
And built ships on the Clyde
And wars, always wars.

At home or firth of the country
We have so much to be proud of.
What a heritage! What a culture to build on!
What a legacy of innovation and creativity!
Science, engineering, medicine, the arts, and humanities
We Scots are an adventurous people,
Curious, creative, energetic and enterprising
Scotland is more than a place
It is a way of life; its people filled with
Passion and commitment
Linked to the world, working in the world

I am a global Scot; at home anywhere
And, as the story goes,
"Where the Scot sits there is the head of the table"
Free in thought and action
"He lives at ease that freely lives"
Unconstrained by place or geography
Unconstrained by ideas or philosophies
Inspired by Scotland's culture and heritage
Inspired to create a future, leading the world

I don't feel oppressed, downtrodden, shackled
I feel free in a land of free thinking
A "man o' independent mind",
Making my mark across the world

In a nation without boundaries
A nation unconfined
No borders to intellectual enlightenment
Creativity and innovation
Open to new ideas
Leading these islands, and the world.
In a nation comfortable with itself
Confident of its future
Clear in its vision
Compassionate and caring, at home and abroad
An interdependent Nation,
Joined with the world by knowledge, trade, economics
The environment, health and people.
Scotland a nation, and in an age
Beyond independence
No borders, no boundaries, no barriers,
No limits. So much to do.
My Scotland.

And it's my Union too!
I am part of it and can influence it
They are my institutions too.
They are my people, my friends
They are part of me
Malachai Malagrowther got it right
Uniformity is not a given in the Union
Scotland can, and is, different
But we have common interest
And common citizenship
The Caledonian antisyzygy still feels right
I can be both Scottish and British
And enjoy and rejoice in it.

In my Scotland
My heritage is my source
My beginning and my nourishing spring
Music, literature, culture, knowledge
But this heritage does not bind me
It liberates me.
Like a river flowing outwards
Linked to wider worlds
Joined by other streams
Not limited like a loch
Nourishing locally, but not beyond
Beyond independence and separatism
My Scotland is a broad river flowing to the world.

I am now back on Arran, the west side
To finish my story in Blackwaterfoot
With its glorious beach, waves lapping my feet
And the oystercatchers crying,
And the best 12 hole golf course in the world
Here lies the authentic Bruce's cave
Where he watched the spider as it tried and tried,
And tried again, to reach its goal.
The metaphor is clear.
It is up to us to keep trying
To make Scotland better
With no boundaries, no borders, no barriers,
No limits; so much still to do
My Scotland.

August 2009

Brookit   — *neglected*
Antisyzygy   — *the coming together of opposites*
Malachai Malagrowther   — *a creation of Walter Scott to retain a Scottish Bank Note*

The Greenwich Sandpit

I was watching the grandchildren playing in the sandpit
Different faces, races, religions, colour and sexes
Playing together in the sand
Helping each other, digging and building castles together
With occasional squabbles and disgruntled faces,
      usually within families
Easily settled
Some real fights and conflicts
In which old people would intervene, and all was settled.

What a good model of working together,
Brothers and sisters, neighbours, friends and strangers
In a place, Greenwich, surrounded north and south
      of the river Thames
By culture, history, learning, commerce, finance and
      government
Play and fun at the heart of it
Mistakes will be made while building castles
But all forgiven and progress made
Greenwich and its meridian, define time and space
And the sandpit says it all.

And Scotland can do the same in its own special sandpit

Greenwich 2017

80

In Response to John McFall

My response to the challenge by Lord McFall to present the message for the unity of the United Kingdom in 45 seconds on the doorstep.

The Flowering of Scotland
I am a proud and passionate Scot
And want the best for my country
The distinctive culture, heritage and values of Scotland
Should be supported and enhanced
Scotland should be a full partner in the UK
With greater control over its own future.
It should promote its values of fairness
Tolerance, community, equality of opportunity and
        education
Scotland benefits from being part of the UK
And can LEAD the UK in a wide range of areas
Science, engineering, medicine, the creative arts
Manufacturing, business and enterprise
As an effective part of the UK, Scotland can play its part
In an increasingly international and interdependent
        world
And in that role to promote
A fairer, more prosperous and peaceful society
I'm in for Scotland.

8 March 2012

"When will we see your likes again?"

This second line of the unofficial Scottish anthem
Recalls a time in the past, when we were invincible,
And Bannockburn was a remarkable victory.
How long did it last? Not long.
From 1314 it lasted until Neville's Cross in 1346
Where David the King was captured and ransomed
Or to 1513 at Flodden field where King James V was killed
Or perhaps to 1603 when James VI agreed the union
   of the crowns.

Fourteenth century Scotland-what was it like?
No real parliament or democracy
Fighting and murder, right up to the top
Land ownership was key, with strong
Links to England, many Scots had huge estates
Education poor, with no universities in Scotland
And ordinary Scots didn't have a look in
Not very inspiring times

So, do I want to return to that?
Were there no other times and people
Other than Bruce and Bannockburn
We would like to see their likes again? How about
The great figures and time of the Enlightenment,
Or Scotland's contribution to health, science, engineering
And the arts-writing, music, architecture and education?
Would they not be better to see their likes again?

The anthem goes on
"Those days are passed now
And in the past they must remain
But we can still rise now
And be the nation again"
Now I agree with that!
Together we can change the world for the better
As we have done in the past

Sometimes it is wrong to look back.
We should look forward. We should create our future
Not live in the past.
So what do we want to be?
How do we see ourselves and our Nation
In the international, Interdependent world we live in?
That's for us to decide — and we will.

On Lewis

First the vision, Sic a sight
Wi' aw the colours, Green, yellow, blue, purple, white.
And then the fragrance and sweetness, everywhere
From the red and white clover, it fills the salt laden air
Of the Machair

And then by the roadside the thistles, bristles swaying
Bringing back memories of the old saying
"Ye can wipe yer bum wi ' a rose or a shamrock
Let's see ye dae it wi ' a thistle."
Scotland's emblem.

I stand here on a misty Lewis beach, replete with mystery
On the far west coast to reflect on early Scottish history.
But why here? Well, why not in Lewis.
I look out to the turquoise sea, across the silver sand
And remembered.

Within the space of a few miles you can see
The Stones of Calanais, four thousand BC
The broch of Carloway,
The Iron age fort at Bosta
And the clearances

The black houses and the white houses
While overhead an aeroplane flies to America,
And from the car I call home on my mobile phone
Six thousand years in a few hours
That's why.

A church founded by the brothers of Columba
And a host of other churches
Many visitors and lang years since
The island briefly visited by the Bonnie Prince
That's why

And the fight for land and kail
The hard soil and the winter gale
The oppression against man and the elements
The struggle for language and freedom
That's why

So in this distant corner of the Nation there is a good story.
A search for Scotland must begin with history
Why are we as a Nation, different from others?
Have we some special ingredient, as a country or as a people
Something which sets us apart.

Here in Lewis we see the roots to the past
The poverty, the repression, the courage
And the love of the land, the language and liberty
The triumvirate which has kept Scotland different
It is in the history.

It is in the stories we remember, the tales
Not the dates, but the heroes we recall, Scots or Gaels
With inaccuracy, but with feeling and emotion
Our memories are tinged with passion
That's real history.

Now, with the heron on its quest for fish, on the dark waters
And the ripples and the waves from the two otters
The story expands as I look out on the loch
The fresh green grass of the summer beckons
As I think of Scotland.

A land has been fought over and died for
A living both poor and bountiful scraped from it.
Rich in resources, coal, oil, wood and water
Rich in its people and their genius
People, the true heart of Scotland

Aeons ago when the earth was a bairn
And the land unformed, yet someone was carin'
To create a wee country with hills and moors
Rivers and Forests, beasts and wee flo'ors
First the rocks were formed, spawning hundreds of theses
On the geology or Arran and Lewis Gneises

Then we went through a series of phases, I can be quite specific
These were the paleo, meso and the Neolithic
This last new stone age, 4-2000 BC
They hunted and gathered and caught fish from the sea
They built dwellings like Scara Brae, real solid stone
They made instruments and ornaments in ivory and bone.

They built chambered tombs in elaborate fashion
Maes Howe for example with its wonderful dragon
They set up standing stones, Calanais
The carved rocks in a cup and ring pattern
They lived in communities and traded here and there
To England and beyond.

And then there are the chess men. A Viking hoard
Found on a beach, if only they could speak and tell us
Of the Estates of Scotland, Kings, Queens, the church
The knights and nobility, and the common people
But playing chess is only a game
Creating Scotland is no' the same.

But they are part of Scotland's history
Love of the land, the language and liberty

The natural world

A green mist

It was the green mist that struck me
As I looked up the glen
It was low down in the trees
Not up in the hills
Sometimes it was green but became orange or white
As the tiny leaves burst from the cold hard wood
And spring and regeneration had begun
A few weeks later the mist had become a sea of green
While two cherry trees, in bright pink raiment
Stood out amidst the green

2013

Autumn Light

The evenings darken and the dawn is delayed
As the autumn unfolds, the skies remain bright
And as the winter days get shorter and the sunsets glorious
A new sight appears in the dark woods
As the leaves fall, the ground is light and luminous
With the freeing of the sky
With a light that will keep bright all winter
And the noon light brightens further with the frost and
snow
And the earth is alive and ready to be renewed again in the
spring
And the plants, waiting for the signal to grow
For everything there is a season
From the dark woods of summer
To the bright woods of winter
Growth and light replacing and re-affirming each other

2012

Birdsong in Tesco's

It was at the cereal shelves that I first noticed the birdsong
Examining the fat and sugar content of Weetabix
I first noticed the chirping
I closed my eyes and heard it more clearly
Sometimes single, sometimes in groups and sometimes in
great swarms
Like the starlings at the Solway Firth
I felt I was at the edge of the forest or in a field of wheat
Birds every where, though I knew I wouldn't see them
I opened my eyes, still at the cereal shelves
And listened again to the tills, whistling and singing.

2 March 2008

Defining Green

Spring at last, sun shining, warm air
And the trees and bushes blossoming.
Greens everywhere, I see from my window and in the park
Silk green, emerald green, satiny, silvery greens
White green, yellow green, lemon green, lime green
Light green, orange green, blue green, red green
Dark greens from the evergreens
Grass green from the lawns
All shapes and textures
A multicoloured green tapestry
Impossible to define, but wonderful to see
A rainbow of greens
And why such a difference
When all the greens come from chlorophyll
And in a few months it will all be yellows and reds.

2008

The empty fag packet

A dull March Morning
Mist on the hill and a cool breeze
With the remnants of snow
Hidden by the swirling clouds
As we walked up the glen
The sky cleared and the burn
Rushing from the top of the hill
Appeared in full flood
Then the lambs, with their mothers
Gambolled across the field
Little flocks of new life
Clean and alive with joy
When we reached the big burn
It was rushing over the stones
Gurgling and splashing while
The trees and bushes on each side
Just beginning to bud with hints of
Green and red everywhere-idyllic
Peaceful and relaxing
It was then I saw the empty fag packet
Discarded as useless and unwanted
Messing up my walk, but
Reminding me of the world out there
Of the noise, the smell, the rubbish
The other part of my other life
Unfortunately I need both

26 March 2011

The snail

The snail appeared on my fingers
As I pulled the weeds,
I popped it on the wall and watched.
I had, inadvertently, put the shell on its back
Slowly, but surely, the snail's snout appeared
And with certainty and without speed
Its body emerged from the shell
It flattened on the wall and without apparent effort
The shell turned over and, off it went,
To eat more of my plants.
No fuss, no meetings, no anger, no noise
It just turned over, and off it went.
Determined to succeed and to make a living.
Not so slow after all.

2 August 2009

The sound of winter

A glorious bright morning and the grass white
    and thick with frost
I looked over the still and seemingly silent field
Where Mungo was playing and rolling in the cold sods
Everything seemed quiet as the light shone through
    the trees behind me.
Then I heard the sound; the sound of the end of autumn
Pit, pat, pitter, patter
In the cloudless sky it could not be rain.
I turned round and saw the yellow and black-spotted
    frozen leaves
Fall from the lime trees and hit the frosted grass with
    a pitter, patter.
They dropped one after another each unique each
    with its own sound
I looked across the field to another group of trees,
    and there was one
Whose base seemed to be filled with a circle of crocuses,
    yellow and bright
Yet these were dead leaves but foretold the spring ahead
In the midst of the sound of winter, and the end of autumn.

2008

To a mouse

On seeing a mouse between the rails at Euston Underground station

Wee, sleekit, cow'rin, tim'rous beastie
There's nae panic in thy breastie
Thou didna start awa sae hasty
In Euston Underground Station
I certainly couldna chase thee
Across the rails.

I watched thee, and saw the train arrive
Nibblin' awa just tae survive
As the Carriages came in
Ye mesmerised my brain
But I could do nothing to help
With you beneath the train

I'm truly sorry man's changing science
Has disrupted your alliance
With nature
And changed the union here
'Tween man and mouse
Deep underground

Your house I glimpsed it in the wall
A tiny hole, but then you're small
And can escape
Your bairnies there, cosy and good
Waiting for you to scrounge for food
From daily commuters

Above the rails and platform, what a story
You see humanity above in all its glory
And what a sicht
Squeezed thegether in an awfu crowd
Reading, eating, talking so loud
Unconcerned wi' you

Am I blest compared wi you
As I board the tube to Waterloo?
On the Northern line
You're warm and fed, and have no computers
And have come to terms with London commuters
I still have some way to go

I have more travels and decisions to take
While you are safe at home, eating discarded cake
And with the family
I have creeping old age, and joints which creak
Hingin' thegether from week to week
And look forward to an uncertain future.

Waves

I often stand on sand or stone
Feeling, watching, listening
To waves, the tide, the foam
The water shimmering, glistening

The waves, powered by wind
Are sometimes loud, boisterous too
Sometimes soft and sensual
Always changing, always fresh and new

The power of these waves is awesome
Eroding grass and stone
Creating sand, grinding soil
The power to smooth and hone

The gentler waves smooth the beach
Lapping softly, a filigree of foam
Bringing calm and thoughts of sleep
Peace to free the mind to roam

The tides, the moon, the source of change
Rising, falling twice a day
Linked to the seasons and to climate
Measuring life in its own way

Sometimes as the tide turns
The ebb lifts small stones from the shores
Their tinkling noise is soothing
This relaxes, calms, restores

Thus a spectrum of power is displayed
From vigorous to gentle persuasion
Both have their time and season
Reflecting leadership and vision

I watch the water ebb and flow
Determined by the tide
I cannot change everything today
Be patient, my time I bide.

2008

Wild life in the West End

It was wet and drizzly.
We were tired and fed up, then
Through the damp and the light rain
Mungo and I could see the two deer
Not far away
They heard us first, then saw us.
They stopped, looked,
Leapt effortlessly away.
Across the tall grass
On the overgrown football pitch.
They stopped again,
And gave a superior glance
At Mungo's bark.
Then off and into the woods
In that west end park
We watched them dissolve
In the mist and the rain
And we walked home, happy again

1 August 2008

The two faces of hawthorn

From the train the hawthorn is spectacular
Bushes white with flowers round fields and trees
Thick fronds which catch in the train's slip stream
As it rushes north, the thorns hidden from view

Now at home the small white flowers are more intense
Pale petals peppered with dark stamen
And now the thorns are visible, sharp, firm, forbidding
The danger now exposed.

It is now autumn, and the white flowers are blood red
Soft and shining but still hiding the thorns.
A promise of a cold winter ahead when the last of the leaves
Have been shed and the full vigour of the thorns at last
revealed

And awaiting spring and renewed growth.

2004

Rhythms

There are rhythms in our bodies
Rhythms on the land
Rhythms in the seasons
Tidal rhythms on the sand

Rhythms in the moon and stars
Rhythms in the sun
Tell us when the day starts
And when the day is done

And there are rhythms in the ferries
As they go from shore to shore
Bringing people, food and packages
And so much more

But rhythms can be disturbed
Arrhythmias you might state
If you think about your heart
It can fibrillate

The seasons can be disruptive
With rain and hail and snow
The tides can sometimes rise too fast
With problems, as we know

And so it is with ferries
When they stop it's such a pain
No bread upon the table
You can search in vain

The letters don't arrive
And the papers delayed
At least we have the tele
To see how Rangers played

The post stops coming through the door
The visitors are late
Can't get to my work
It will have to wait

But then it starts again
Cardioversion not required
Back to sinus rhythm
And then the bills arrived.

So how did it end?

From a Photograph from James Cassels 12.3.11

Bird photo of the week on Arran

The photograph was remarkable
A high speed film had captured the two birds
The first, from above, was a kestrel
His talons fastened on the tail feathers
Of the second bird, a barn owl.
Both caught locked together
In a life threatening tussle.

But the camera stopped there;
It was not clear what the outcome might be.
Would it be a sad ending, the power of the kestrel
Pulling the owl down, finishing it off.
Or perhaps a happier one, a few feathers lost
And escape into the night, like Meg losing her tail
In Tam O'Shanter.

But happier for whom? The Kestrel or the owl?
Both need freedom, both need to reproduce
And live. The barn owl eats the mice and rats
The kestrel larger prey. Which one should die?
If you had the power of life or death,
What would the next picture show?
You choose.

27 March 2011

Quality of life

The sly young fox sat, and from across the road
Watching Mungo on a wet February night.
Mungo on old flatcoat, shiny and black in the rain
The fox cocked its head as Mungo barked
Randomly and hysterically.
The eyes of the fox were caught in the light of a passing car.
Mungo gave up, eventually
And shambled back to the gate
With his grey beard and his arthritis.
The fox crossed the road towards him and lay down
Observing the dog, safe behind the fence
Its white chest highlighted by the moonlight.
Though disgruntled and diminished, Mungo knew,
He knew, he was returning to a warm house
Food and company, safe and secure, and the television.
What's a little humiliation compared to that?
And what will the fox do when it is old?
His life is one of adventure, free.
He would not wish to be tethered and spoon fed
His quality of life is different, no pension or welfare state.
Tomorrow night they will meet again, same ritual, same
standoff.
What if they were like Caesar and Luath, the "twa dugs"?
What would they say to each other?
Who has the best life?

2009

The bridge over the River Cloy

"This is the bridge over the river Cloy", I said
Augustus looked, shrugged and just nodded his head
As if to say "Some Bridge", and not too strong
"And the Cloy's just a burn, and not very long"

Augustus, friends, listens to my thinking
He's just a heron, so responds by nods and winking
It's true I confessed, it's just a wee burn
You can almost jump it, when the tide's on the turn

But it's my wee burn and it runs to the shore
Augustus just nods, 'cause he's heard this before.
I looked over the bridge and out to the bay
Ahead is Goatfell, and more snow on the way

The mountain, reflected in the glistening cold stream
Acting as a mirror, it seemed like a dream
Already the hills are white, Chir Mhor and the Saddle
I look back to where the burn begins, too cold to paddle

Back through the woods and homes and fields
And forward to the Castle and the beach and the seals
Small families of ducks on the surface they skim
Feeding and breaking the ice as they swim

Drifting smoke rising from the woods so near
You can almost smell on a day so clear.
The burn has a course and a purpose, to get to the sea
It can change course a little but not the final outcome you see

Augustus agrees as he searches for fish
He is focussed on feeding and if he gets his wish
The burn would continue to meander its way
From mountain and glen and out to the bay

My course is more varied and has changed with time
But the end is the same as my personal hill I climb.

Written on a sunny winter morning 2012

The hardest winter for 60 years

The hardest winter for 60 years
Snow and ice on road and hill
Low temperatures unrecognised
And yet life goes on still

As the ice melts and the snow clears
And through the frozen grass at first unseen
The first shoots of life appear
Snowdrops flourish, firm and green

A sign of spring, a sign of life
Nature it seems, can cope
The seasons come, the seasons go
Everything has a time for hope

Life goes on, the natural order
The chaffinches and the robins need their feed
Rhododendron's form small red buds
The blackbird sings a cry of need

And the world is alive again
A few days ago, mid January and minus 6 degrees
The grass now looks fresh and green
And the buds appear on our apple trees

And the mornings are lighter
And the nights get shorter
Perhaps there will be another summer
Nature predicts it. It will get hotter

And a blink of sunshine and warmth
Opens up the world again

2010

My family

Three wee weans

Three wee weans in the back of the car
They don't know how long how far
 We've travelled today

Three wee weans surrounded by litter
Sweets and crisp pokes, submerge the sitter
We've collected to day

Three wee weans who all need a wash
Stained by ice cream, sweeties and squash
We've eaten today

Three wee weans, in spite of the stress
Look just like angels, I guess
It's been a wonderful day

Three wee weans who have argued and fought
About trivial things and what we have bought
On our journey today

These three wee weans, look exhausted I know,
But at 6.00am tomorrow, they'll be on the go
It's another day,

Three wee weans in the back of the car
They don't know how long how far
We've travelled today

Probably late 1970s

A beetle fell into her bra

Written after a very public incident

A beetle fell into her bra
What a fuss-what a hoo ha
She tried in vain to get it out
I just laughed and I shouldn't have

We turned the cups upside down, inside out
Tried to find the pest
We were in such a public place
People looked distressed

And still I laughed and smiled
And she seemed even more upset
And said, what if a beetle dropped in your pants
Then you would surely fret

We both laughed, replaced the cups
Smoothed clothes, but paid no heed
To the crowd still looking on in awe
And we trotted off at speed.

And then a spider spent the night
In the trouser of her jeans
As she put her foot into the leg
The spider woke and assessed the scene

A delicate set of toes approached
Red varnish on the nails
He scampered out on to the floor
She uttered screams and wails

Poor spider shot beneath the bed
Safe at last he thought
She calmed down eventually
But what a fright the spider got.

Such encounters with insects, rare they may be
Can occur whatever the weather
And in spite of the problems, as you can see
They've brought us much closer together.

Clearing up after Mungo

The kitchen was the first place
Dog biscuits, other food, dishes and toys
Littered debris and smelly towels
Floor swept and washed and black hair removed

The long hall took longer
The hoovering took the time
And picking up the toys and outside the bathroom
Where he drank and lay, needing special attention

Lounge and dining room took little time
But the den where he slept and
Beside our bed where he lay
Will need proper cleaning

It was the study which hit me
My own room where he lay beside me
And I stroked his handsome head
That I found it, between the shredder and the bookcase

It was.... his duck
Chewed, yellow feet torn off
Holes in it and ragged
But it was his

He brought it to the door when we came in
He took it to the kennels
He laid his head on it
And we played with it, pulling it til it ripped even more

Unlike the others I couldn't throw it out
Discard it for ever
I will keep it in a special place
In Brodick where he loved the sea

I knew where he would be on Brodick
He swam for hours no matter the temperature or the wind
Swimming with the swans and seals
Alive and happy

As I will remember him, and his duck.

2009

Moving house

In just a few days-soon to be hours
I will leave my home, its garden and flowers
For thirty years it has been a rock
A magnet, a polestar to which I have returned
On high days and sad days
And always for succour and support

For months now the clearance has occurred
Book, toys, clothes; the pictures become blurred
In black bags, boxes and skips
They were all sent to their last resting place
Each weekend and holiday
Continual blood letting of my past.

Rooms look empty, shelves tidy, books collected
House cleared, all in order, ready to be inspected.
But it is not my house, no disorder
Too clinical, less human than it was.
The slow removal of my soul
And the replacement of my daemon.

I will miss my home, not just the bricks and mortar
But as part of me, my wife, dogs, son and daughters
Birthdays, festivals, celebrations, sadness
Squabbles, arguments, tears, laughter
Happy, loving, hateful, angry
But mine, my place, my life.

But I will look forward, and create a new place
My house, my home, my books, my space
A place of rest, family events
The renewal of traditions and the annual cycle
A return to the rock
An anchor which will hold

20 May 2004

What will you remember?

What will you remember
Of your first holiday on Arran?
The beach, the sea, the shells
You, at 2 years old, collected?
The painting, with brushes,
And with hand and foot
The apples in the garden
The baby swallows being fed
And Ailsa, our little beagle,
And the fun you had.
Ailsa your best friend.
Swimming in the sea and the pool
Playing in the play barn
Walking in tiny pink wellies
And jumping in muddy puddles
The toys we played with
And the games we enjoyed
Picking pretty flowers
The bathing and sleeping routine
Sun hats and sun creams
And the midges!
When we returned to Glasgow
We bathed and washed your hair
Water spilling every where
With the swimming frog I bought.
Reading stories with you, I learned a lot
The books we read, as your little hands
Turned the pages and you remembered the words.
I hope this has begun, in you

A fascination with books,
With reading and story telling.
Before I placed you in your cot
I held your hand as you fell asleep
Breathing gently and at ease
The next morning in the flat
You walked Ailsa along the hall
Holding her lead in your tiny hand
And your cheeky wee face.
After our last wee cuddle
I said I loved you so much
And then the car was packed
And we said goodbye
Both of us with a tear in our eye
And when you got home and you phoned
And said "I love you so much"

I hope you remember as you grow old
What we did and enjoyed.
I will not forget these weeks together.

August 2014 after 2 weeks on Arran and in Glasgow with Grace

From the Top of the Tower to the Top of the world

I was at the top of the Tower
Re-opened at last
I could see across Glasgow
Both present and past

I looked over the City
Its buildings, open spaces
I recognised so much
Some favourite places

Football stadia, tower blocks
And the broad river Clyde
Not as busy nowadays
But still dark and wide

The University of Glasgow
High on Gilmorehill
The Kelvin flowing through the park
Yet all seemed still

To the north I see Ben Lomond
The Dumgoyne and the Campsie hills
To the south Goatfell on Arran
And the old Paisley Mills

I phoned home to my wife
To describe the delights
She had declined to rise,
Her fear of Heights

She told me she had spoken
To my newly pregnant daughter
Who had been to the clinic
For a scan, as is proper.

And then she let me know
That the baby's sex was clear
In quiet tones I asked, well what?
The answer was, a boy my dear

I was on top of the tower
And now on top of the world
A boy to join wee Grace
The hairs on my head began to to curl

I was in tears and speechless
So happy I cried with joy
What more could a grandfather want
Than a girl and a boy

A wee brother for Grace – Brodie

July 2014

Preparation and anticipation

The fourth floor of a store in London
unseasonably warm on a March Saturday
the floor full of pregnant ladies —
just like an antenatal clinic, but
with grannies, aunties, children
as well as husbands
the products are amazing and
so different from 40 years ago.
Prams replaced by buggies of all sorts
feeding dishes and microwave sterilisers
undreamt of years ago.
And what they do with nappies is amazing
hair washing dishes, and bath thermometers
no need for elbow testing of the bath
toys and playthings, washing mats and
baths of all shapes and sizes

and the anticipation.
Expectations of the birth ahead
the joy the happiness and the pain
names being considered
and discarded and compared.

A big Squeeze of Love

Some people like a cuddle
I like to have an embrace
Others like to have a hug
But not my granddaughter Grace.
   She has a "Big Squeeze of Love"

She likes to hold my hand
When I read her stories at night
Or as we gather shells upon the beach
And watch the stars at night
   And she gives me a squeeze of Love

We draw and we play
Build castles, and make pools
Play with brother Brodie on the mat
But it's Grace who writes the rules
   And she gives him a big squeeze of love

And we take Ailsa for a walk
Grace takes her by the lead
As we walk up the Glen
Little treats she likes to feed
   And the dog gets a big squeeze of love

It's such a simple thing to do
A cuddle, hug, embrace
Yet it means so much to me
And I love you Grace
   When I get a big squeeze of love.

Index of first lines